Running is just Happiness

"A happy life is just a string of happy moments. But most people don't allow the happy moment, because they're so busy trying to get a happy life." – Abraham[1]

---

[1] www.facebook.com/Abraham.Hicks

Running is just Happiness

Poems for Runners

Steve McCloud

Lulu Press

Sydney

2014

ISBN 978-1-291-68160-4

For all Runners

Much appreciation goes to...
Karmea Fitness and 2XU Running Crew

Acknowledgements

With special thanks to Sarah Anne and Warren Evans from Karmea Fitness – Integrated Coaching for Performance and Life.

Thanks also to the 2XU Running Crew:
Derek and Kaye, Simone, Di, Ian, Jackie, Joseph, Yasmin, Andrew, and Bronte.

Included are all the awesome runners from the Thursday night runs with Karmea at Manly Beach, NSW.

Running together with a group of positive, determined and focused runners has been the inspiration for these poems.

Table of Contents

Running is just happiness

A group of twenty
Social jogging
Warming up
Ready to rumble
Intervals again
From Manly Surf Club
Onward to North Steyne
Shoulder to shoulder
With Sarah Anne
Surge ahead
Or fall behind
Both feet in mid air
Defy gravity
How good it feels
To run with tribe

Run faster than time
Leave the past behind
Run toward the future

The what ifs
The how it should be
Fall by the way

Run toward open sky
The blustery wind
A taste of ocean spray
Knee joints in rotation
Hips swinging in unison
Running is just happiness

Quiet the footfall
Run tall
The indigo moon
Is beaming down
Lengthen the stride
Pick up the cadence
A burst of vitality
Make a move

Let the mind stretch out
From the training gains
The strength drills and the sweat
A new self belief is blossoming

Turn the heart
Toward starlight
It feels so right
Capture it
Make a photo
Or just let it go
And start over
Fast free flow
However it turns out
Will be a win

Run faster than time
Leave the past behind
Run toward the future

The work and responsibilities
The what ifs
The how it should be
Fall by the way
Run toward open sky
Surge ahead
Or fall behind
How good it feels
Both feet in mid air
Defy gravity
How good it feels
To run with tribe

The power of running

Is primal, basic, urgent
From here to there
A breathe out, a stride forward
The mid foot striking the ground
Leaning forward from the ankles
in eager expectation
Of rhythm, ease, efficiency
A visceral grace
Of muscles and tendons
The focus is purposefully forward
The heart pumps the blood
And the lungs fill with oxygen
A rush of energy
To the top of the hill
When thought dissipates
There will be a moment of Zen
A cathartic release
From the daily pressure
Alignment, fitness

A surge brought on
Through a force of will
The euphoria
Will be worth the effort
Just open the front door
And step onto the path
Run in unison with others
Speed, momentum, buoyancy
White summer clouds racing
Across a blue sky
There will be a power of you
In the midst of running
The power is
Just as the wind moves

Kick up the River

When the way is long
When that old rusty gate is locked
When time has you submit
And the air burns your lungs
You just got to…

Throw the trash
Kick it up
Kick it down
Make a splash
Pick a color
Run strong
Give it all
Kick on
Kick it
Mix it through
Take the hit
Shift the shit
Spill it

There's a hitch
At the gate
Lost the ticket
Take it on
You the Kong
Punching through
Give it voice
Left right
Show your fight

Power it
Pick up the heel
Give it heart
Scratch the itch
Kick it up
Kick it down
Take it on
To the Treasure
Make it steel

Show your metal
Push the pedal
Colt 45
Energize
Just allow
KAPOW!!!

Make it right
Blow your light
Kick it up
Kick it down
Make a splash
Throw the trash
Pick a color
Do it now
Run strong
Be a giver
Be a fighter
Kick up the River

You can do it
Nothing to it
Take a breath

And you said you never new how…

Long distance lone solitary

Against better choices
Despite the steamy summer heat
Through the storms of self doubt
Into the pelting rain and thunder
Where the pressing wind pushes back
When a mates in the lounge
With his feet up
On the sofa

I am into the running
Like a wolf on the trail
Snow falling in the stillness
The trail leading on
Through Christmas tree forests
Far from southern shopping centers
With their buzzing air conditioners
Eyes like icy pools
Ablaze with fire

Through a glitter of white
Toward the birthing twilight
Relaxed across the shoulders
Easy in the paws
Stealing deep breaths
Running just for the joy of it
All sweat and instinct
A pelt of steam and crystals
The stamina to keep strong
Along this way of wilderness
A test of bone and sinew
Making deep tracks upon
A chilled silent magenta sky
The pace quickens
And with wilful intensity
The power of wolf
Is leading to home

The running is easy

The running is free

This is the song

Of the long distance lone solitary

When the wild howl from inside

Takes you forward

The warrior of hill sprints

There will be War
Or chocolate cake

Run up that hill
Everything will feel alright
Flowers will bloom again
There will be serendipity
Time to take a lover
Just that little bit
Of extra effort
To succeed

One foot in front of the other
Rhythmic of cadence
Leaning from the ankles
Pick up the heels
Determined at the beginning
Keeping focus to the end
At the summit

Standing tall
Hold the dream
Take command
The warrior of hill sprints
Defiant and fearsome
Standing proud

There will be War
Or chocolate cake

Take it easy
Or take on that hill

Make fire in the rain

I'm a little boy again
Innocent of sin
Laid still upon the grass
Still upon the grass
Let us run the Sky together
Reach beyond the Stars
I want to tell you how
How my wonder will take me home
When will we find home

The soul is traveling
There is no journey greater
Than the one I am on

Lift me skyward Father
Let us pray together
I will run on
Until my heart gives out
And the end of my running

Will be when I know
That death is no more
That life is as it should be
For the living
For the victory

Mother I must tell you
There is a joy in agility
The child in me
Freely flowing forward
Just for the fun of it
I want to tell you how
My wonder will take me home
When will we find home

Grounded and focused
A commander I have become
With a stern course
And a military strategy

Each skill I learn
Builds upon the last
Supple and balanced
And dexterous of mind

Give it everything
Run faster than you can
The sky will burst
And a God will meet you
With open arms
Each footfall creates a spark
Make fire in the rain
We must find a way
For *that old rusty gate* to open

We are the sacred runners
We who run fast with grace
We who have the endurance
We who run with courage

Great Mother and Father

Let us pass through

Surrender

"There is only one perfect road
And that road is ahead of you
Always ahead of you"
Sri Chinmoy[2]

Running on
Close your eyes
Take on trust
Imagine a path
Just ahead of you
You will not know
The map contours
Or the place markers
You have a gun
With no bullets
There is a ghost
At the next turn
A hole at your feet

---

[2] www.au.srichinmoyraces.org

A feeling you cannot express
Will you stumble?
Or will you stride on?
Close your eyes
Take on trust
Running fresh
Running true
Imagine a path
Just ahead of you
You will not know
And no-one can show you
Which way to go
Just imperfectly
Surrender

Stay young forever

Don't ever get old
Take all the pills
Walk your talk
Keep fit keep loose
Keep running keep on
Throw a finger
At death
Know that you can
And that you must
Live eternally young

A physical rigor is necessary
For the leopard out back
To run free and fast
Rekindle the ardor of cells
Tend to the fluids
With always kindness
Be rid of the parasites
Shift it with spells

Speak it true
Revel in it
Run it down

Stay young forever
Don't ever get old
Take all the pills
Throw a finger at death
Know life is good
Just as you made it
Baby just as you made it

Honoring the ancestors

The granddads, the grandmothers,
Aunts and uncles
Time has laid them to rest
So I can be here now

It doesn't matter
The running technique
First or last
There will be time enough
I cross the line to honor them
And I know they are with me in spirit
Cheering and applauding me on

I am the fulcrum of their hopes and dreams
All my strength
All my breathe
All my heart
I cross the line for them
For just a moment

In-completes

Are rendered complete

Flowers freely growing

Within an open field

The love that was held

At last received and known

First stirrings of the morning breeze

Gifts given back

Such fragrant colors

Gratitude

In the midst of summer rain

To teleport

From here to there
Is just a mental balancing trick
The two hemispheres in sync
A third circle into focus
Opening a portal
Instantaneous
A flash of magic
The atoms just follow
The light dreamer's dream

Running was never this easy
Start by imagining
Crossing the finish
Before the race has begun
Surprise your colleagues
When you show up
In two places at once
From there to here
Here now, within, quietly

Running to the finish

Running to the finish
Will there ever be an end
A completeness and resolution
The shining wholeness
An earth angel

Running to the finish
Will there be a cup of glory
A holy grail to possess
Or just persistence
When the legs hurt
A quiet satisfaction
In making it across

Running to the finish
All the wounds and worries
The mistakes and hard knocks
Cannot quell the spirit
Running to the finish

Only the one thought is needed
I can do this
So that in looking back
Striped bare
I can see myself clearly

How my eyes caught the morning sunlight
How my expression held resolute
How my body in alignment
Crossed over the line
How I smiled in joy
And with great relief
Dropped to the ground
To rest and get back my breath

That old rusty gate

"…May your unfailing love be with us
Even as we put our hope in you"
Psalm 33[3]

Running up that hill
How many times now
And with such vivacity

Never give up
Self discipline
Determination
Positive focus
Strength of purpose
Soul thriving
Revision into
Reworked vision
Divisive demons
Dissolve into oxygen

---

[3] Holy Bible – New International Version

Energy levels increase
Circles within circles
Within circles

Me and you
You and me

Hold my hand a moment
Look into my eyes
Love is flowing out
Light dancing on the water
Hush now

That old rusty gate

The one that's locked from inside
Into the dreams of the fallen
Is creaking slowly open

Aspire to greatness

Do it even if you don't have time
If you don't have the money right now
If you feel tired and worn down
If the world is getting the better of you
If your cars broken down
If things just aren't turning out well
If your shoulders are tense
If it's raining and cold
And you just want to cry

Quietly aspire
One step in front of the other
No need to fuss
Hold to trust
It will turn out right
Take a breath
Find a way
You will be greatness
You will be loved

Open the door

Run on

Afterword

It is so much fun being part of a running group – I enjoy the social camaraderie as well as being extended competitively during the training sessions. I have been able to refine my technique, pick up the pace, and join with fellow runners of all levels toward a shared positive goal.

My running style, technique, and efficiency have all improved from being coached by Karmea. With their support I have been able to gradually integrate the changes to my running form and as a consequence running now feels much easier and I have more speed with less effort.

With consistent practice I have seen an increase in my stamina, strength and endurance and I have been able to lower my finish times across 5k, 10k, and 14k events. I also include complementary activities such as pilates, surfing, cardio workouts, meditation, and writing as part of my program.

I experience a great sense of freedom from running and it empowers me to release the stresses of modern living and generate good feeling neurotransmitters such as endorphins. Recent research has shown that two key factors in life extension include a calorie restricted diet and interval running. Intervals include short bursts of intense running with equivalent periods of slow jog recovery. I have found these to be very effective in increasing my fitness level and I have gained confidence in running at a faster pace for a longer period.

I consider running to be a great test of character, fortitude, and mental attitude. Beyond this there have been Zen times in the midst of running during an event when I have transitioned beyond the personal self and discovered a new level of awareness and effortless flow.

I offer these short poems as encouragement and inspiration toward your running practice. I suggest that you set some quiet or meditation time aside to imagine a vision of your end result, what you want to achieve from your activity – whether it's crossing the finish line victorious or just running free and happy with friends.

LIVE KARMEA LIFE

A truly integrated approach to your fitness, well-being & performance

www.karmeafitness.com

THE HUB Building 2, North Head Sanctuary, 33 North Head Scenic Drive, Manly, NSW 2095

www.facebook.com/steve.mccloud.7

www.2xu.com.au/rungroup/

www.ingramcontent.com/pod-product-compliance
Ingram Content Group UK Ltd.
Pitfield, Milton Keynes, MK11 3LW, UK
UKHW020215250726
13967UKWH00001B/13

9 781291 681604